Let's Talk About...

Life 101

By Angela C. Williams

Let's Talk About...

2

Life 101

By Angela C. Williams

Copyright © 2018

ISBN-13: 9781986715669
ISBN-10: 1986715663

Dedication

To Myself

Angela C. Williams

Table of contents

I. Family
Page 6

II. Finance
Page 8

III. Education
Page 10

IV. Health
Page 12

V. Friendship and Teamwork
Page 15

VI. Goals and Hobbies
Page 17

VII. Love
Page 18

VIII. Sex
Page 19

VIIII. Death
Page20

X. Peacefulness
Page 22

I. Family

Family is very important. There are many different family structures in society. The strength lies in the commitment given to each person involved, within each situation or incident in his or her life. Rather you believe that a family is always supposed to be a father, mother and children or not. I think we can all agree that a family should be there for one another in some way. Rather it's financially, spiritually, physically, or on pen and paper.

Where your parents are from and how they were raised, is vital. Where and how they choose to raise you can be colossal. Understanding one another; brother, sister, mom and dad; and communicating regularly has to flow like water. It's not easy. But, we have to work at it, get outside help if necessary; to make it effective and easier.

When there is not a brother or sister, having a friend in your age group, who is very close to your family; is great.

Celebrating birthdays and having occasional family gatherings are memories made that can carry us through tough times. Taking pictures and making scrapbooks of happy times, may serve as a stress reliever when life gets overwhelming.

It's key that we understand that it can still be "a good birthday" without a party. There are many ways to celebrate a birthday. Even when we can't be with immediate family. Even when we don't have enough money to do exactly what we'd like.

Consistency is important. But when there is a lack thereof: divorce; abandonment; moving around frequently and/or a loss of employment or another life altering event occurs; we must find a way to keep moving forward. Surrounding ourselves with positive people can prove helpful. When we can't surround ourselves with positive people. We need to be sure not to surround ourselves with those headed in the wrong direction.

It is extremely important for us to ask questions and volunteer information about or families past. As the child it is important to understand the limits in which our own parents may have regarding guiding our lives. Finance and education play a key role in that process. I'm not sure which is more devastating. Education without finance or finance without education. (A college degree without a well-paying job or a well-paying job without a college a education).

II. Finance

How our parents earn their money and whether they have money or not, may dictate our paths to a certain extent. If they have a college degree, chances are greater that they will earn more and/or be more prepared to guide you. Some parents believe in allowance, some don't; whether they have money or not. If they have the money but don't explain to you that you need to, and show you how to, save your money; giving allowance may backfire.

If your parents have a career that stems from a college education, most likely you will too. Understanding that you need to work and finding a way to stay employed is detrimental.

Understanding that a profitable business, can flourish from a trade; is paramount. But understanding how to create a strategy to grow a business through clients, sometimes takes a lot of wit and a lot of time. Within the world of business, there must be an understanding of savings, credit and loans. Even outside of that field, the understanding of financial discipline is pertinent. Try your best to save your money.

Once you have decided what career you would like to pursue, then you can decide how to go about educating yourself. Finding financing for your education may be another quest if there is no college fund.

Family is also important so that we all may always have shelter. Even when we are mentally ill and need medication. Better we deal with them than the police if at all possible. It's a catch 22. How do you take care of a person who has a record and can't work? (Let's make an effort to get our grown sons/daughters and American Veterans, off the street. No one should be homeless.

III. Education

Education starts when we are very young. If we see our parents read, cook and clean; chances are, we will read cook and clean as well. Rather it's the bible, a magazine, or a novel. It can never be a bad habit to pick-up anything and read it. Even if you don't agree with the item being read. You may need to further analyze the item to prepare yourself for a future debate with someone who tries to persuade you in a direction in which you are unsure.

Parental guidance in pre-school is a must. They need to learn, play and grow. That will incorporate reading, fun and culture. Oh yeah, and eating too.

It is my hope and prayer that our elementary teachers find a way to make learning fun at an early age. Finding a way to keep the children's attention can steer them in one direction over another, I believe. Staying focused can become a challenge.

Thinking and planning for your future education beyond grade school should not be taken lightly. It's crucial. Teens; talk to everyone you know about what they're planning to do. Share ideas. It's much easier now. Just Google it ☺.

Making friends and learning to plan, work and coexist well with peers, classmates, room-mates and co-workers is a beast.

Parents must be involved in daily homework assignments. Even if there extent of involvement is just asking do you have homework and have you completed it. Periodically that parent should leave a message for all of their child's teachers, inquiring about his/her grades. The other parent's may need to use the internet to get a better understanding of their child's particular chapter assignment. Even then; encourage and celebrate accomplishments with your child.

As we grow, we must understand that we may be stronger in some areas than we are in others. Constructive criticism can be helpful from all those concerned. Especially friends.

IV. Health

Often, what our parents do, cook and eat or drink is what we continue to do and eat or drink, as well. If they never change their health habits, sometimes, nor do we. In which case we will all suffer the consequences. Sometimes it can be unclear just what is good for our bodies and what is not. Sometimes it's not hard to know. Like alcohol, cigarettes and drugs. Don't start and you won't have to worry about stopping. Exercise your spirit, mind and body. (Hang around the right people). Keep up with health trends. Talk to your doctors. Read Health magazines; eating/drinking what you know is not bad for you and keeping yourself safe, is the answer for longevity.

I suppose in an ideal world, we could all plan to have a family exercise day and time. Say; after dinner. With all that everyone may be involved in, it's challenging to just join one-another at the dinner table. Afterward it's back to your personal focus. You cannot give up on finding personal time to exercise. Always take a multi-vitamin. (Beginning at age 3).

Spiritual and mental health works cohesively with your body's physical health. Board games that help us think, remember and be creative; exercise our minds. Having a personal hobby can, not only relax your mind but it can lead you down a road that may help to bring in extra income.

Whatever your spiritual belief. If it keeps you centered and well, then so be it. If it's not working; study a few other methods that help you center yourself (and not become a menace to others). And yes, we all need help in one way or another. Some more than others.

When trauma from accidents, war or abuse effect our minds, the situation of finding peak mental and physical health, can be exacerbated. Whether, it's time to heal concussions or medicine to counteract a chemical imbalance; doctors are here to help. Friends and family are supposed to be there for us but that may not always be the case.

From grade school on, we all deal with some form of verbal or physical harassment at some point. Finding those who are educated or sane, and understand that neither physical nor verbal harassment are ever appropriate, may make the situation better. Unfortunately; often times we have to excuse ourselves from the non-sense. It is my hope and prayer, teen-agers; that you never have to leave school or a job due to harassment of any sort.

V. Friendship / Teamwork

We all know that classroom/lab group assignments and work projects between co-workers won't necessarily bring new friends; however, each of these situations respectively, requires organization, maturity, and give and take.

Just like education, friendship and teamwork begin when we are very young. Our first friend may be a neighbor, class-mate or team-mate, but each is just as special.

Having friends or team-mates is imperative but what you choose to do with them is the key. Parents must pay close attention to what their children are doing. At every age. They must also be sure to incorporate culture in the fun/games and leisure time. It would be good to allow your child to visit other homes to see other parenting styles; to have dinner and to maybe sleep over when it is appropriate.

Although finances may cause involvement in the activities to be limited. In one place or the other; community, school, church or work; eventually activities should be offered for free. No matter your age group. It's never too late. Dance, sports, roller-skating or writing poetry. Stay involved and stay active. It leads to a healthy life-style. Once your good health is gone; sometimes it's too late.
It is important that parents find time to support children who have joined clubs and are participating. Make the time. If they need to practice alone with you; make the time. Coaches may serve as great references down the road. The habits we form as youth, don't usually depart from us completely, if we chose to do them.

VI. Goals / Hobbies

From planning your own birthday party to getting a high school project completed. Maybe choosing a college; or Finding a hobby. Maybe you need to lose weight or change your eating habits permanently. You may be planning on a strategy to win your next game. Make a list of your skills. Know where your skills are needed. Organize your thoughts. Ask questions and do a little research. Ask your friends, family and co-workers what they think you're strong area are. Where do they see the most talent in you? Maybe you need to find financing. Whatever you're working on; set a goal. You can set goals at work, at school at home or for leisure events. Set these goals so that you can plan and succeed at becoming the best, you can possibly be.

A hobby can be fun, educational and may even earn you income. You may even end up joining a club of like members who enjoy the same thing.

At the end of the day, you have to wake up and look at yourself I the mirror; reflecting on all of the decisions you've made.

VII. Love

I suppose everyone has a definition of love in their mind. But even then, that doesn't mean that they love everyone or even most people. That doesn't even stand to say that they love themselves. When we love ourselves; not the situation or the money we have; then we can be at peace to truly love others. Your self-love will be up and down and up and down, if it's based on 'stuff', situations or how you are treated by people.

When I say, "Are you trying to find someone to love or are you loving those who find you"? What do you think I mean?.....................
Are you showing kindness and love to every man woman and child in your path or are you on a quest to find friends who have the same amount of money as you?

If you ask yourself the question; do I love those I come in contact with, as I love myself? What do you think your answer would be? In most cases? Only you can and should judge, you. Ask yourself. How do you make other's lives better? Do you make anyone's life, worse? Who's made your life better? Who's made it worse? Most of the time when you believe in a higher power; you believe in loving unconditionally. Do you love unconditionally? Do those around you seem to love you unconditionally?

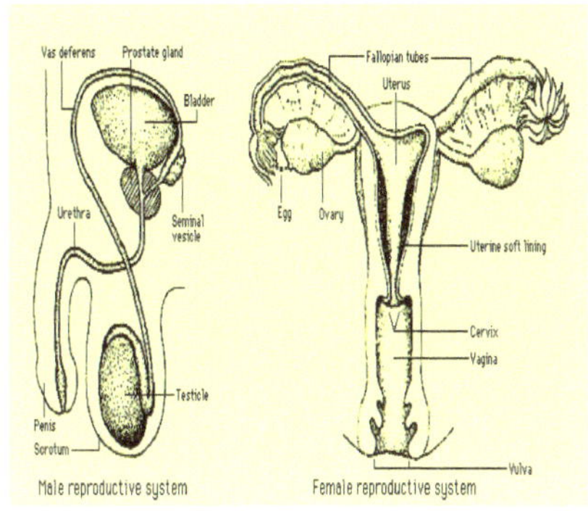

VIII. Sex

Sex is something that is very natural. It is necessary to sustain life. Unfortunately when it happens between two people who are not ready mentally, emotionally or financially; it becomes an enormous problem for a lot of people. From widespread disease to a broken family and maybe even a child being raised in poverty. From Chlamydia, Gonorrhea, Hepatitis, Herpes; to HIV which leads to AIDS.

Whether you're gay, bi-sexual, lesbian or you believe in heterosexual marriage and monogamy; from spreading disease, breaking hearts and promises through misleading information, to dividing an innocent child between two households. They are all situations that are unhealthy.

Sex is meant for marriage and reproduction. I apologize if you do not agree. I believe we all should try our best to keep sex within marriage and to keep baby making to the married couple as well.

IX. Death

We wonder why our friends and loved ones had to go when we hear that death has befallen them. Well, no one lives forever on this earth. Preparing ourselves for that day may make it easier to accept. Helping someone else through his or her life, may help them to accept their own death and help us to accept their death as well. Knowing that you made a difference. Everyone doesn't have the same fortune. Sometimes those who are more fortunate need to give more. Give to those who are trying and to those who are in situations where those around and able to help, choose not to. Helping someone less fortunate, to find a family; to make friends; to have a chance at healthcare; to set attainable goals; to manage their income; and how to love unconditionally; is invaluable. Encouraging and showing him or her how; not having sex until he or she is married, is the best thing for all parties involved. Including the unborn child.

Are your priorities out of order? Maybe you are not a part of the solution because you are part of the problem. Don't be complacent! Put on your giving gloves, your happy shirt; your thoughtful hat. Smile, hug and give until it hurts.

Unfortunately, the way that a person dies is never easy to handle: sudden death, due to bad health- stemming from poor eating habits; accidental death by someone who drank too much and chose to drive anyway; a long-term debilitating ailment that just appeared and had no cure; or a vengeful murder that left you speechless. It's difficult to understand. Sometimes it's difficult to continue day to day. Pastors, ministers and peer groups can all be helpful. But sometimes we just need a kind word from a friend or a concerned stranger.

X. Peacefulness

Life is what is happening around us and pretty much, to us as we go on day to day; right where we are. The ghetto; the gated community; or in Hollywood. When we are at peace inside of ourselves, we will spread peace. When we are at war inside of ourselves, we will spread war. When we are sick, we will spread sickness. When we are ignorant, we will spread ignorance. No matter where we live; or work; or play. No matter how much money you have.

A visit to the library, is free. The zoo, is free. Most museums, are free. The park, is free- (a frisbee, a football, a kite etc.

I love you. Love me back.

John 3:16 Check it out; in the Holy Bible.

Conclusion

Sorry dad. I apologize to all of those who I offended in my first adult, fiction book. (The material was sexually explicit at one point). Please stop harassing me on my job and in the Library and in the doctor's office and in the grocery store and in the park. Since you refuse to purchase my books, I have no other means of income except for my regular job. I am not a whore nor did I use to be. Please do not harass my child or grandchild. Thank you in advance.

I write because it is my passion. I have a degree in Mass Communications. I'm an author. I love Jesus.

24

Thank you to:

It.wikibooks.org
Englishferdinandofeliu.blogspot
freedomrings1776
flickr.com
aibert.blogspot
elgar.blog
hoichigenchem.wikispace
sunshine.reflections.wordpress
yr8science2011.wikispaces
inam.net